iPod Fan Book
Go Everywhere with iPod

PRINT HISTORY

| August 2004: | First Edition. |
| September 2004: | Revised and updated. |

iPod
Fan Book

iPod Fan Book
Go Everywhere with iPod

by Yasukuni Notomi
translated by Aya Brokering-Iwata

ENGLISH EDITION

Editors:	Philip Dangler
	Molly Wood
Technical Editor:	Eliot van Buskirk
Cover Designer:	Ellie Volckhausen
Production Designer:	Emma Colby
Interior Designers:	David Futato
	Melanie Wang
Illustrators:	Robert Romano
	Jessamyn Read
Proofreader:	Genevieve d'Entremont
Indexer:	Julie Hawks
Contributor:	J.D. Biersdorfer

JAPANESE EDITION

Editor:	Masayuki Yamamoto
Art Direction:	Hiroshi Nakajima
Design:	Kana Sugai
	Takuro Kumamoto
Photographs:	Plank Co., Ltd.
Photography Advisor:	Tatsuya Yusa

ISBN: 0-596-00776-0
[L]

[10/04]

Contents

iPod
Fan Book

Preface

The iPod Fan Book

Long ago, people decided they wanted to listen to their favorite music at any time and in any place. This desire led Sony to develop their groundbreaking portable cassette player, the Walkman. Since then, portable music players have evolved and sound quality has improved. It's no longer unusual to see people walking on the street while listening to music. We're now completely accustomed to carrying music around to various places—on airplanes or trains, at school, in the office—and enjoying it in any number of situations.

With the introduction of the iPod, Apple completely changed the portable music industry. Before the iPod, you could travel with only a small portion of the music (as well as digital audio books, radio programs, and voice recordings) you wanted to hear. But thanks to the massive storage capacity of most iPods, you can now take your entire audio library out for a walk.

The iPod has created a legion of users sporting distinctive white headphones, and people are as passionate about their iPods as they are about the music they choose to play on them. The iPod has become more than a music player—it's become a lifestyle.

Hence, the *iPod Fan Book*. Originally published in Japan, this book examines the iPod as an integral part of your technology lifestyle. Although we've translated it for you, our English-speaking readers, we've tried to retain some of its Japanese sensibility and hope this will help you see the iPod for what it is—a truly global phenomenon.

What makes an iPod an iPod

The iPod is a tool that puts many kinds of "sound" media, starting with music, into its small body and lets you play and enjoy them at any time. For this reason, the iPod includes many useful functions, such as the ability to easily load music from CDs or listen to your music in a certain order. The iPod alone cannot record music or allow many people to listen to music at the same time, but it has many features that will enhance your individual listening experience.

Music is a fundamentally personal media, and what the iPod delivers is more than just a few tunes—rather, it creates a unique environment for listening to sound. To use the iPod to its fullest potential, you must listen to lots of music. Luckily, there is no audio player more convenient than the iPod. Its most remarkable feature is that it allows you to carry such a huge volume of music in your pocket.

The iPod's other main attraction is its sheer simplicity of use. At first, you should not concern yourself with anything other than listening to music. If you're just starting out, the following paragraphs will get you up to speed—later in this book you'll find many useful tips for mastering the iPod's music player capabilities and using it for other tasks as well.

Preface

Recording
Guide

iPod on
the Go

The Power
of Playlists

Music
Distribution

Tips and
Tricks

iPod
Accessories

Additional
Resources

iPod
Fan Book

X

iPod generations

Which iPod do you have?

In this book, we'll cover general iPod usage tips, so it won't really matter which version you have. In the following pages, however, we'll look at the many generations of iPod and clearly explain the differences between them. At the heart of it, however, an iPod is an iPod no matter what the design. They all help you enjoy your music and take it with you wherever you go!

The original iPods

The very first generation of 5GB iPods—Mac-only and released in 2001—feature a 2" (diagonal) screen above a mechanical scroll wheel. This wheel is surrounded by four separate arc-shaped navigational buttons. The top arc is used to access the menu, the left and right halves are used to rewind and fast forward, and the bottom arc is used for the play and pause functions. In the middle is a slightly raised select button, used for menu selection. Apple announced a 10GB version of the original iPod in March of 2002, followed by a 20GB version in July. These revised second-generation iPods featured a wired remote, thinner FireWire cable, a carrying case, and, most notably, support for Windows.

Third-generation iPods

The third generation of "dockable" iPods was released in April of 2003. In addition to the dock, these much thinner 3G models introduced a touch-sensitive scroll wheel. Originally sold in 10, 15, and 30GB sizes, Apple later updated the line to 10, 20, and 40GB, then upgraded the low-end model to 15GB after introducing the iPod Mini.

If you look at the front of the dockable iPod, you will see four round touch buttons under the screen. These buttons are the "forward/rewind" button, the "menu" button, the "play/pause" button, and the "next/fast-forward" button. As with the original iPods, the scroll pad and select button (in the middle) are used to navigate and select all menu options.

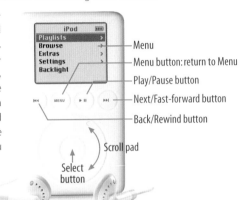

Menu
Menu button: return to Menu
Play/Pause button
Next/Fast-forward button
Back/Rewind button
Scroll pad
Select button

Preface

Recording
Guide

iPod on
the Go

The Power
of Playlists

Music
Distribution

Tips and
Tricks

iPod
Accessories

Additional
Resources

iPod
Fan Book

The iPod Mini

In early 2004, Apple introduced a new type of iPod: the iPod Mini, which uses a tiny one-inch hard drive to store 4GB of music. It comes in five colors of anodized aluminum, and features the first incarnation of the Click Wheel with included buttons. It weighs a mere 3.6 ounces and is smaller than most cell phones!

The add-on FireWire and USB 2.0 (for Windows computers) dock ($39) makes it easy to charge your Mini and sync it to your computer. It also contains an audio line out port, which will allow you to connect to powered computer speakers or a home stereo.

The tiny size, durable construction, and sportiness of the iPod Mini often inspires techno-lust, even among those who already own iPods! If you simply must have one, you can justify your purchase by pointing out that the Mini is (obviously) smaller, and easy to carry in a pocket. And yes, they are quite stylish, but this book will also show you how practical the purchase of a Mini can be.

For starters, you can use the iPod Mini as your gym music player (just make sure to use the included belt clip or optional armband to minimize shock on the treadmill or while jogging). Later, we'll talk about how multiple iPods make it easier to keep all of your music organized.

The Click Wheel iPod

After seeing the success of the Click Wheel in the iPod MIni, Apple decided it had a hit on its hands and released 20 ($299) and 40GB ($399) white versions of the Click Wheel iPod in July of 2004. But the iPod engineers didn't stop there. The latest version of iPod also features a much-improved battery life of 12 hours (up from the previously advertised 8), the ability to shuffle songs from the main menu, and the option to save multiple "On-The-Go Playlists" (more on these and other playlists in Chapter 3). It allows syncing and charging via the included FireWire and USB 2.0 cables, and contains support for more languages. All this, plus it's slightly thinner and weighs only 5.6 ounces!

iPod
Fan Book

iPod connections

Connecting and disconnecting the iPod

The iPod connects to a computer with the
provided iPod FireWire connector cable.
You can also use the iPod Dock, which is
provided with some models (see the list
on page xv for details). Once the iPod
is connected to a computer, iTunes will
launch and transfer your music library and
playlists to the iPod. To disconnect, click
the Eject button in iTunes.

Power adapter and
charging

The iPod comes with a power adapter, and
will automatically charge whenever it's
connected to a Mac or Windows machine
equipped with a 6-pin IEEE 1394 (FireWire)
port. In the newest models, you may also
charge and connect to your iPod with the
included USB 2.0 cable, but charging takes
slightly longer using this method.

iPod checklist

Here are some of the primary differences between various versions of the iPod:

Buttons

The most recent iPods (Minis and white) are buttonless, while the dockable iPod has four buttons right below the main screen. Original iPods have mechanical buttons incorporated into the scroll wheel.

Size and weight

They're all small, but the iPod has steadily decreased in both overall size and weight. The Minis are the smallest, weighing at just 3.6 ounces. The original iPods tilt the scale at 6.5 ounces, while the newest 40GB models weigh just a bit less (6.2 ounces).

Connectors

All iPods come with a FireWire port and a standard headphone jack. USB ports were introduced in April 2003 and are standard on all subsequent models.

Docking

The dock was also introduced in the April 2003 revisions. Docks are currently sold separately for the Mini and 20GB Click Wheel models, but included with the 40GB model.

Additional features

The newest iPods have many other additional features: they display more song data (number of times played, ratings, etc.), include a Clock function with time zones and an alarm function that can play music, allow multiple On-The-Go iPod Playlists, let you customize the main menu, display text files with the Notes feature, and are equipped with three new games: Solitaire, Parachute, and Music Quiz.

Recording Guide

iPod Fan Book

Your empty iPod

Without music, your lovely little iPod is nothing but an expensive portable hard disk. Only the addition of music turns it into the tool we call *iPod*.

You probably know already that you can't record music directly onto the iPod. First, you have to transfer music from CDs and other sources onto your computer and, from there, onto your iPod. This system is a little more powerful than, say, plopping a CD into a portable player. However, it presents its fair share of inconveniences—ranging from incompatible files to organizing all those tunes. Here's some handy advice for getting music onto your iPod and avoiding common problems.

Not all sound files are iPod-friendly

There are some sounds on your computer that you won't want to transfer to your iPod, such as sound effects collections for video editing and audio creation, karaoke tracks, or presentations. Sometimes this music is saved on your computer in formats that can be played on the iPod, so it's important to figure out how to prevent those sounds from automatically being transferred (more on that a little later).

Got space?

Say you've just bought a new 40GB iPod and want to fill it with your music, but don't currently have any of that music on your computer. Before you start ripping your entire CD collection (or buying songs from iTunes willy-nilly), remember that you'll also need at least 30GB of empty disk space on your Mac. If possible, it's best to use a dedicated hard disk for music, such as an external FireWire hard drive of 60GB or more. Such drives are relatively cheap these days, and they let you expand your digital music collection without interfering with your other computing activities.

Leave some space

Sure, the iPod's main job is to store and play music, but it can also function as an external hard disk, storing all kinds of data—from address book contacts to documents to spreadsheets to videos. That's very handy if you want to transfer a bit of data to another computer. So think about putting aside a couple of gigabytes of extra space for pure storage—you might even consider buying an iPod with more memory than you think you need.

Don't worry: nothing's set in stone

It's ultra-easy to change the music on your iPod, so don't fuss over what music you transfer. The excuse "I won't listen to it so much" doesn't make sense with the iPod. Besides, if you bought the CD, chances are you'll want to hear the songs on it at some point. That's one of the strongest arguments for the iPod: there's enough space for songs that are only tangentially interesting to you. You can always delete them later.

Getting music from the Internet

The iPod can play any MP3 file, no matter where it comes from. So you can get tunes from various kinds of music sources from the Internet—not just from CDs.

There are a variety of sites where you can download MP3s. Among them are MP3.com (*http://www.mp3.com*), Emusic.com (*http://www.emusic.com*, which is pay-per-download), download.com (*http://music.download.com*), Insound.com (*http://www.insound.com*), and Epitonic.com (*http://www.epitonic.com*). Of course, another popular option is to buy songs right within iTunes, from Apple's iTunes Music Store. Just click the Music Store icon in the left pane of iTunes (Version 4 or later has the store built-in) and you can browse for songs and entire albums, create an account, and purchase songs for download with just a few clicks. It's a very simple process, and most songs in the huge catalog cost only 99 cents apiece.

Preface

Recording
Guide

iPod on
the Go

The Power
of Playlists

Music
Distribution

Tips and
Tricks

iPod
Accessories

Additional
Resources

iPod
Fan Book

4

Using iTunes with Windows

One of the most significant boosts to the iPod's popularity was the introduction of iTunes for Windows. By the fall of 2003, the iPod and iTunes were by far the most popular audio combination on the block. But Windows users weren't totally satisfied: they had a PC-compatible iPod, but its integration with MusicMatch left much to be desired. Finally, though, Apple released iTunes for Windows, which looks and works almost the same way as the Mac version.

If you currently use MusicMatch Jukebox with your Windows iPod, it's easy to switch over to iTunes. You'll find that it makes downloading music and organizing your iPod much easier. Just download iTunes for Windows from Apple (*http://www.apple.com/ itunes/download/*) and follow the installation instructions. You can use both iTunes and MusicMatch on the same computer, but the bottom line is that the iPod works better with iTunes. Therefore, it's a good idea to let Apple's application handle your music— you'll avoid any file compatibility problems because everything you encode from CD (for example) will be in iPod-compatible MP3 or AAC format.

Incidentally, once you install iTunes, the connection between the iPod and the PC will be automatically controlled by iTunes. You can keep using other programs such as Music-Match and Audible Manager (for audio books from Audible.com), but you cannot use them to synchronize data with the iPod. If you find that you're no longer using third-party tools, it's fine to delete them.

Importing your existing library

If you didn't import your library when you installed iTunes, you can simply drag and drop music folders and files onto the iTunes Library icon. Under Windows, these files and folders should be easy to find, since most software automatically saves it to your My Music folder (Start → Documents → My Documents → My Music, or just double-click the My Documents folder on your desktop).

You'll probably also want to import your playlists into iTunes. You can't drag and drop a playlist, but most Windows audio software will let you export playlists in M3U format. In MusicMatch, just click File → Export Playlist Tracks and select the "Copy as is" option. This will save the playlist wherever you've specified. You can then click File → Import (or press Ctrl-Shift-O) and choose the folder where you saved the playlist. Be sure to specify under "Files of type" that you want M3U files.

Preface

Recording Guide

iPod on the Go

The Power of Playlists

Music Distribution

Tips and Tricks

iPod Accessories

Additional Resources

iPod Fan Book

Here's another tip. Before you start importing your music, click Edit → Preferences → Advanced, and check the boxes next to "Keep iTunes Music Folder organized" and "Copy files to the iTunes Music folder when adding to library." Then, once you've imported the music, click Advanced → Consolidate library. These steps will copy all the music on your computer into the iTunes Music folder, so you can delete the old files and neatly organize all your music in one place.

Switching your iPod to Windows

Thanks to iTunes for Windows, it's actually easy to switch from using your iPod with a Mac to using it with a PC. You'll just need to reformat the iPod the way you would a hard drive. Here's how. First, with the iPod plugged into iTunes, click the iPod icon and check the box next to "Enable disk use." This option allows you to use the iPod as a portable disk and to manually update songs and playlists. Next, you'll need to download the iPod Software for Windows updater from *http://www.apple.com/ipod/download/*. Start the installation, follow the onscreen instructions (there's more than one update in the file, so be sure to install the proper version of the software for your iPod), and restart your machine. After rebooting, select Start → iPod → System Software → Update.

Once the update starts, connect the iPod. (Make sure the battery is fully charged, because the iPod will not draw power from a PC the way it does from a Mac.) This should bring up the iPod Updater screen. Click "Restore" to erase the iPod and reconfigure it for the PC.

> You will not be able to transfer your music to the PC before you erase the iPod, so be sure to back up the music to CDs or some other format.

iTunes and iPod

If you use a Mac (or Windows, and have followed the previous instructions), you know that iTunes and the iPod are inseparable. So, we'll start with the basic methods of using iTunes to obtain, organize, and transfer music to the iPod. The point here isn't really to show you how to use iTunes, but you'll probably learn a little along the way.

Loading CDs with iTunes

❶

❶ When you start iTunes and put a CD into the drive, iTunes connects to the Internet and automatically obtains song information for each tune on the CD, from the CDDB database (*http://www.gracenote.com/gn_products/cddb.html*). While some CDs don't show up in the online database, a vast majority of them are listed, which saves you the trouble of manually keying in the Artist, Album, Genre, and so on.

❷ The complete data for an album shows up after you right-click (Windows) or Control-click (Mac) the CD on iTunes' left side and choose "Get Info" from the menu. Here, you can rewrite the song data to create your own music organization system or doctor song titles to your fancy.

You can also create rules for renaming songs and altering song data. We suggest using a genre and name of the artist, etc., to conform to your own organizational rules. For example, you can change *John Mellencamp* to *John Cougar Mellencamp* and label the specific genre as Classic Rock, rather than the more generic Rock genre. (If you find yourself bored with similar sounding tunes, you may actually want to add Generic Rock as a category.)

❸

❸ If you click the Import button at the upper-right corner of the screen, iTunes begins to copy the music on the CD onto your hard drive and encode it into the format of your choice (the default settings work well, especially if you plan to use your music only on the iPod). If your CD-ROM drive is fast, importing takes about five to eight minutes per CD.

❹ To change settings for ripping (copying music from) CDs, click iTunes → Preferences → Importing on the Mac (or Edit → Preferences → Importing on the PC).

❹

Sending music to the iPod

① The music from the CDs you rip is registered in the iTunes Library. If there are any tunes you don't want to transfer to the iPod, uncheck the box to the left of the song name. In this example, we've decided not to transfer a long "song" that's actually a whole album.

② If you right-click (Windows) or Control-click (Macintosh) a song in iTunes and choose Get Info, you'll see an information screen for each song. In addition to adding detailed song information or associating an image with the song, you can turn the volume of each song up or down, alter the equalizer settings, or set when you want the song to begin or end. These sound settings are applied to the songs as they transfer to the iPod. It's a handy feature when the volume of the original tune is much lower or higher than your other tunes, or when you know you'll want to hear a particular song with more bass or treble.

③ When you connect the iPod to your computer, a screen appears asking you how you want the music transfer to take place. By clicking the iPod button in the lower-right corner the screen, you can call this screen up at any time.

Preface

Recording Guide

iPod on the Go

The Power of Playlists

Music Distribution

Tips and Tricks

iPod Accessories

Additional Resources

You can set the music transfer method here, choosing whether you want the iTunes and iPod data to be synchronized automatically (Automatic update), or to transfer only the songs you choose. Automatic update is the easiest method, but if you want to make sure you don't put any other sound files on your iPod by accident, try adding songs, artists, albums, and playlists one by one, or use Playlist Syncing. Playlist Syncing is also a good idea if you have more music than you have space on your iPod, since you can make sure the size of the playlist to be synced never exceeds the amount of disk space on your iPod.

❹ If you've chosen to add music manually, you can use iTunes to delete songs from your iPod when it's plugged in. Choose the iPod icon from the list marked "Source" on the left side of the iTunes screen. Select a song and press the Delete key or click Edit ▸ Clear.

❺ To make sure songs that you've deleted don't get loaded again the next time you update your iPod, be sure to uncheck the box next to any songs you don't want. After doing so, you can select Automatic update and the deselected songs will no longer be transferred.

Song Name		Time	Artist	
☑ Sk8er Boi	○	3:24	Avril Lavigne	○
☑ I'm With You	○	3:43	Avril Lavigne	○
☑ Mobile	○	3:31	Avril Lavigne	○
☐ Unwanted	○	3:41	Avril Lavigne	○
☑ Tomorrow	○	3:48	Avril Lavigne	○
☑ Anything But Ordinary	○	4:11	Avril Lavigne	○

❺

The right rip

By default, any CDs you rip using iTunes are encoded in AAC (Advanced Audio Codec) format, which, according to many, produces better sound from smaller files (i.e., at a lower bit rate) than MP3. However, you can use different formats, and depending on the type of music you're copying, you'll probably want to. We recommend ripping most music to MP3, since that format is compatible with the widest array of software and hardware. Here's how to choose the right ripping method for a few different types of music.

Ripping rhythm-based music

The MP3 format is far from ideal for "ricky-tick" music such as techno, Euro beat, or music that expresses the rhythm with waves of bass (certain types of dance music, for example). If you encode such music at a low bit rate, you can end up with a *sh-sh-sh* noise—these sounds are artifacts left over from the MP3 format's inability to properly handle certain frequencies. Make sure you rip such music at bit rates greater than 160 kbps (128 kbps is considered the minimum for good sound). You can change bit rate settings by clicking iTunes → Preferences → Importing. Under Settings, choose Custom, and then choose your bit rate from the drop-down list.

Ripping melody-based music

Since the iPod was designed primarily with headphone listening in mind, you probably won't be able to tell the difference between a midrange-heavy song (something without lots of bass, cymbals, or acoustic instruments) ripped at 128 kbps and the same song ripped at 160 kbps. Therefore, to save disk space, feel free to rip such music at 128 kbps when using the MP3 format. If you're using the default AAC format, you can probably go as low as 96 kbps.

Ripping tone-based music

In the case of music with many multilayered, differentiated elements (piano or violin solos, psychedelic music, choral music, etc.), you want to make sure the tone quality of the instruments comes through clearly. For this highest level of quality, you could rip your CDs to the WAV format (Windows) or AIFF format (Macintosh), without compressing it to MP3 or AAC. But if you did that, you'd run out of disk space pretty quickly. A better option is to use the Apple Lossless Encoder, which was added in iTunes 4.5. This option provides the quality of uncompressed CD audio, but uses about half the storage space.

However, the best compromise for such sonically demanding music is VBR (Variable Bit Rate), which encodes the music with variable compressibility depending on the complexity of a given sound. With the right VBR, you can re-create a very rich tone while keeping an MP3's file size small. Note that iTunes does not have a specific setting for AAC VBR ripping, although Apple says that all of its AAC encoding is done at a VBR.

Ripping spoken-word CDs

Sometimes you might not be ripping music, but *spoken-word* CDs—say, audio books, stand-up comedians, correspondence courses, or dramatic readings. In that case, don't waste your time (or hard disk space) on a high bit rate. Even 96 kbps might be too good for certain spoken-word recordings. We recommend using the AAC format at an even lower bit rate. If you're using iTunes (other apps don't rip to AAC), an AAC at a bit rate of 64 kbps is ample for most spoken-word files.

Ripping CDs without track gaps

The iPod can't skip from one song to the next without inserting a small amount of silence. Most of the time it's no big deal, but when you're listening to live albums, the gaps between tracks can be annoying.

You can keep live performances intact by clicking Advanced → Join CD Tracks after inserting the disc to be ripped into your drive. iTunes will then rip the CD as one long track. This can make it tough to rewind and fast-forward to find a specific song from the CD, but using the iPod's scroll wheel helps a lot.

Other than that, you could also use the fade in/out function on your iPod so that you aren't irritated when the blank between tunes is suddenly cut. This is better for people who place importance on the shift between tunes, rather than trying to eliminate gaps between tracks.

A note on bit rates

When you rip songs from CD to your computer using a compression format such as MP3 or AAC, the factor that determines the quality of sound is the *bit rate*.

In short, the bit rate reflects how much data is used per second of the song. For example, the default bit rate configuration of iTunes is *160 kbps* (kilobits per second), meaning that 160 kilobits of data are consumed per second. Since bit rate corresponds roughly to the amount of information sent in one second (in this case, the amount of music data), the bigger the number, the better the file will sound. As you might have guessed, larger bit rates also mean that the resulting file will take up more disk space. A well-balanced setting is somewhere between 128 and 160 kbps.

Uncompressed audio has an equivalent bit rate of 1.3 Mbps (big M for *megabytes*), so if you choose a bit rate of 128 kbps, the resulting file size will be one-tenth that of the original file. Compression formats such as MP3 or AAC generally strike a good balance between compression rate and quality of sound, though AAC sounds better than MP3 at the same bit rate because it's a more advanced format.

VBR, or *variable bit rate*, is technology that varies the bit rate depending on the sonic characteristics of each part of the song you're encoding. VBR encoding automatically uses a low bit rate for parts that don't require high-quality sound, and high bit rate settings for parts that demand it. It typically sets maximum and minimum bit rates, and then varies the bit rate between them. This way, the encoder can keep the sound quality relatively high, while minimizing file capacity. Still, you should be careful when using VBR—the technology can sometimes lead to larger file sizes without a significant increase in sound quality.

iPod
Fan Book

iPod Quick Tip

Rip CDs the lazy way

If you have a big collection of compact discs already, you probably want to put a lot of them on your iPod. But ripping a whole stack of CDs at once can be very boring and can take up a lot of mouse clicks unless you let iTunes do most of the work for you. You just have to set up your iTunes preferences the right way.

On a Mac, go to iTunes → Preferences → General (on a PC, choose Edit → Preferences → General). Next to "On CD Insert," click on the pop-up menu and select "Import Songs and Eject." Then click OK. Now all you have to do is keep putting CDs in the computer drive and iTunes takes over. It downloads the song titles from the Internet, imports the music and ejects the CD by itself, all without you having to do anything!

Preface

Recording
Guide

iPod on
the Go

The Power
of Playlists

Music
Distribution

Tips and
Tricks

iPod
Accessories

Additional
Resources

iPod
Fan Book

16

Recording Internet radio

Sure, iTunes has a great built-in online music store, but the Internet also offers a plethora of radio stations that broadcast music from all periods and cultures. If you record some of these Internet radio programs to your iPod, they'll provide hours of music for your portable listening pleasure.

Recording complete radio programs

For the Mac, you can capture audio with an Internet radio recording tool such as the free Stream-Ripper X (*http://streamripperx.sourceforge.net/*), which you can use in collaboration with iTunes. On a PC, use Total Recorder ($11.95, *http://www. highcriteria.com/*) to record your favorite shows.

One quick caveat: you can't improve the sound quality of Net radio that was broadcast with a low bit rate. Many stations broadcast their programs at 56 kbps or less, so whenever possible, choose a station that broadcasts with at least 128 kbps.

Extracting your favorite tunes from broadcasts

We think the best way to enjoy recorded Net radio files is to simply play them on your iPod, sort of like a delayed cable broadcast. But many people may prefer to cut out tunes from the recorded file and listen to them individually. On a Mac, your best bet is to use QuickTime Pro to edit the file. For PC users, we recommend using Audacity (a free program that also has a Mac version), available at *http://audacity.sourceforge.net*. Either program allows you to open the recorded file and divide it into several parts. Just choose the part you want to isolate and save it as a new file, or, if you want to keep most of the program as a chunk, delete the part you don't want and save the rest.

Get analog tunes onto your iPod

Once you enter the digital music world, you'll probably want to listen to your old records or cassettes. How can you get that music onto your computer, much less on your iPod? Here are several ways to do it.

Necessary devices and connections

Before you can listen to albums on your iPod, you first need to get the sound from the records' vinyl grooves onto your computer. In order to do so, you'll need an audio interface that can convert from analog to digital. You could use your computer's sound card, but that technique typically adds a fair amount of computer noise to your recordings. Griffin Technology's iMic is an excellent recording device that costs less than $30. It works on both Macs and PCs, and simply plugs into a USB port. The iMic is bus-powered (so it doesn't need an external power source) and it's extremely easy to use. Mac users who buy an iMic also get Final Vinyl—free software that makes it easy to record from tapes and records, and then edit and clean up the recordings. Or, once again, both PC and Mac users can use Audacity (as we do in the following example).

You can just connect the computer to the analog sound source by way of an audio interface (the iMic or your sound card). It's simple to play the record and push the record button in your software, just as you would with a traditional cassette recorder.

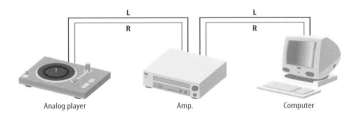

Analog player   Amp.   Computer

If you're using a record player for a component stereo, be sure to connect your amplifier between the record player and the audio interface—otherwise, your recordings will be far too quiet and may have other sound quality problems. With a record player that has attached speakers (i.e., one with an integrated amp), it's fine to connect directly.

Analog recording

Once the hardware is connected, it's time to fire up your recording software of choice and get ready to record. There are many options out there for Windows, and since the sound quality depends on your hardware, you can use whichever program suits your needs. Just make sure to use something that has recording level meters. As mentioned, Audacity is a good choice because it's free, offers plenty of editing choices, and includes a noise removal feature ⑧ for cleaning up your sound. On the Mac, you can also use Final Vinyl for free (if you have the iMic), or Apple's GarageBand. Here are some general directions for analog recording; for specific help with your software, check the program's Help file.

Ⓐ

❶ Start up your waveform editing software (Audacity, Final Vinyl, or Garage-Band).

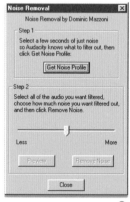

Ⓑ

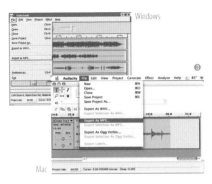

Windows

Mac

❷ Play the desired record on the record player and set the recording level while watching the level meter. The meters should *never* reach 0 dB and go into the red, unless you prefer your recordings besmirched by ugly digital distortion.

❸ Once the recording level is set, you can start recording. It's usually best to record one side of a record album (or tape) all at once. Just hit the record button in your software, then start the record or tape player. When the recording is done, stop the player first, and then stop the recording software. You can then export the long file to WAV, MP3, or Ogg Vorbis (the last option is an open source sound format that the iPod cannot play).

❹ You can export the file directly to your iTunes library by saving it to Music → iTunes → iTunes Music.

❺ It's easy to divide the recorded file into individual tracks. Simply select songs by clicking and dragging over them on the timeline (you can usually tell where one track ends and the other begins by looking at the flat parts of the level meter), then choose an export format and save location for your selection from the File menu.

Preface

**Recording
Guide**

iPod on
the Go

The Power
of Playlists

Music
Distribution

Tips and
Tricks

iPod
Accessories

Additional
Resources

iPod
Fan Book

20

Enjoy DVD soundtracks on your iPod

The music industry hasn't had complete success adding copyright protection to CDs. As a result, many companies are planning to release new albums in DVD format, which has had built-in copyright protection from the beginning. If there's no significant price difference, many buyers might prefer music with video footage to music alone. And since music on DVD is difficult to copy, expect the music industry to strongly promote this protected format. In particular, more and more unreleased live recordings are being sold only on DVD—recordings you might want to put on your iPod!

Copying DVD audio is a tricky proposition. Most of the copy protections for DVDs are divided into two types: one guards against digital copying (CSS), and the other blocks analog copying (Macrovision). However, both types of copyright protection apply only to video footage—*not the sound*. Removing the copyright protection from DVDs is illegal, but there is no need to circumvent that protection in order to record from the audio soundtrack.

Recording sound from a DVD is nowhere near as easy as ripping a CD, but there are tools for the job, and it's getting much easier. If you own a DVD-ROM drive and learn the procedure, you can grab the sound easily and quickly—in fact, you can do the whole thing using freeware. Since you extract audio by DVD chapter, you can also get your favorite tunes from a live-performance DVD. Or, you can grab the soundtracks of entire movies, record them as one file, and transfer them to your iPod. If you're into movie soundtracks, it pays to know this procedure.

Note, though, that DVDs often carry a lower data quality than CD sound sources, so you might hear some decrease in sound quality when compared to that of CDs.

Recording DVD music on a PC

There are two software programs you should use when recording DVDs: DVD Decrypter (*http://www.dvddecrypter.com/*) to copy media files from a DVD to your computer, and DVD2AVI (*http://arbor.ee.ntu.edu.tw/?jackei/dvd2avi/*), which extracts the audio from the DVD file. Make sure to download the English language plug-in as well, and put it in the same directory as DVD2AVI. Finally, you'll need to convert the resulting WAV file to MP3 and then transfer the audio file or files to your iPod. Here are the steps for the entire process:

❶ First, insert a DVD into your PC's DVD drive. If the video or music starts playing automatically, stop it, and then launch DVD Decrypter. Specify the location where the program should save extracted files by typing the pathname in the "Destination" section.

❷ In the panel on the right side of the program, select the chapter that contains the audio you want to extract, and deselect the other tracks. Then click the "DVD to hard drive" symbol on the lower-left of the screen. Loading will start. Try to download only one chapter at a time if possible—even though it's troublesome, downloading individual chapters saves you from redoing the entire extraction just because something goes wrong in a specific chapter.

❸ Once the files are extracted, launch DVD2AVI and choose File → Open.

❹ The downloaded files will be in VOB format. Select them, and then, in DVD2AVI, click Audio → Output Method → Decode to WAV.

❺ Now click File → Save Project, select a destination for the audio file, and click the button to save it.

❻ Now that the WAV file is finally saved to your hard drive, the next order of business is converting it to a format recognized by your iPod. Open the file in iTunes and click Advanced → Convert Selection to AAC to save the WAV in AAC format (assuming that you haven't changed the default encoder). If you'd prefer to have it in MP3, change the "Import Using" setting in the Edit → Preferences → Importing menu.

Preface

**Recording
Guide**

iPod on
the Go

The Power
of Playlists

Music
Distribution

Tips and
Tricks

iPod
Accessories

Additional
Resources

iPod
Fan Book

22

Recording DVD music on a Mac

On a Mac, you'll need software called OSEx (*http://www.cs.buffalo.edu/~afaversa/*) for extracting the DVD tracks, and a52decX (*http://homepage1.nifty.com/~toku/software_ en.html#a52decX*) to convert the audio files. You can then use iTunes to convert the files to MP3. Here are the steps:

❶ First, insert a DVD into your Mac's DVD drive. If the video or music starts playing automatically, stop it, and then launch OSEx. Select the chapter that contains the songs you'd like to download by clicking the "Ch" button, and remove the other check marks.

❷ Click the "Fmt." button and choose "Prog. Streams" from the menu. Then, click the "Aud" button and choose the audio tracks you want. For music, there is usually only one track, but for movies, you could see several tracks, perhaps in different languages. Click the "Begin" button to decide where to save the file, and it will start copying.

❸ After that, launch a52decX. On the drop-down menus underneath the main interface, set Track to "0" and Output to "Stereo."

❹ In a52decX, choose File ⟶ Open and find the VOB files that OSEx created. a52decX will begin converting the files.

❺ a52decX will create an AIFF file in the same folder as the VOB files. You can use Quick-Time Player or other audio playback software to preview the file; if you don't find any problems with it, just load it into iTunes and convert it to MP3 or AAC (as described in item 5 on the previous page).

Optimizing sound quality

There are many programs other than iTunes that let you convert files to MP3. If you use these well, you might be able to come away with a better sounding MP3 than you would with iTunes. Here's why.

Understanding the encoder

The *encoder* we're referring to here is software that is used to convert uncompressed files obtained from music CDs to compressed formats such as MP3.

Some people may tell you that it doesn't matter what you use to encode music, but actually, the quality of sound varies widely depending on the encoder, simply because the encoder's performance is also variable.

For this reason, some maniacal audiophiles even include the name of the encoder in their files to make it clear which encoder was used. There are popular encoders and unpopular encoders among this crowd, and opinions are often subjective, so it's tough to recommend a specific format. Suffice it to say, however, that some people *really* don't think iTunes is the best encoder out there.

Alternative encoders

First things first. iTunes rips CDs on its own, but without an MP3 codec, it wouldn't be able to turn the ripped songs into MP3s. The codec embedded in iTunes is called *Fraunhofer*. However, most experts these days believe the open source LAME codec delivers better sound. There are many CD ripping programs that can encode with the LAME method on both Macs and PCs.

The sound quality difference between different encoders is not always clear. The LAME and IIS codecs seem to be the most popular, but you'll simply have to judge which method sounds best to you.

Be careful not to listen and compare encoders too seriously, because you'll end up realizing that uncompressed AIFF or WAV files sound best of all! If this dawns on you, just remember that you'd only be able to fit about 50 CDs onto the 30GB iPod if you didn't compress your files. (A compression of 192 kbps puts almost 500 CDs onto the same iPod.) Music compression is what makes the iPod so powerful, although it also means that the iPod isn't particularly well suited for audiophiles with $20,000 stereo systems.

The LAME codec consists only of the encoding engine—meaning you can't use it without host software. Since you can't swap LAME into iTunes, you'll have to look elsewhere in order to give it a try. Remember: if you decide to use an external program to encode your MP3s, you can still import them into iTunes—and onto the iPod from there. Here's how to give the free, cutting-edge LAME a try on either Windows or Mac machines.

Ripping with LAME on Windows

For ripping to MP3 using LAME, we recommend a free program called Exact Audio Copy (*http://exactaudiocopy.de*). When you install the program, it will scan your hard drive for the LAME codec, which EAC uses to make MP3s. If EAC can't find LAME, you'll need to download it from one of the sites specified in the setup screen. You can also search Google for "download lameenc.dll". Even if you have the LAME codec installed, you may still want to update it: at press time, the latest (and therefore best, in the case of a codec) version is 3.96. If you want to use a different codec or upgrade to a newer version of LAME, just click EAC → Compression options → External Compression, and click the Browse button. ❶ Now that EAC and LAME have been properly introduced, click the MP3 button ❷ and you're off to the races.

❶

❷

Changing encoders on a Mac

MP3s encoded with iTunes' Fraunhofer MP3 codec sound fine, but again, many prefer the sound of the LAME codec. The iTunes-LAME Encoder (produced by Blacktree, Inc.) works great for this, and is very simple to use.

① Download the iTunes-LAME Encoder from *http://blacktree.com/apps/iTunes-LAME/*. Double-click the downloaded disk image to mount it on the desktop. Double-click the image to open it.

② Drop iTunes-LAME onto the Home → Library → iTunes → Scripts folder on your hard drive to complete the installation.

③ Start iTunes and insert the CD to be ripped into the drive. Choose "Import with LAME" from the AppleScripts menu.

④ Encoding ensues after you click the "Import" button. The default encoding is 184 kbps at a variable bit rate (for more on VBR, see the sidebar on page 13). The process takes a bit longer than a usual iTunes import, but you may find that the improved sound quality is worth the wait.

⑤ By default, the songs are placed in iTunes, where you can categorize them as you would any other song. You can change the save location by pressing the "Prefs" button in iTunes-LAME.

④

⑤

iPod on the Go

2

Obviously, the point of the iPod is to enjoy music or other audio on the go, or to transport files from one place to another. In a word, this device is *mobile*. Sure, you can just pick up and go right out of the box, but you should consider a few key features if you want the smoothest mobile experience possible.

- Output devices (usually headphones)
- Bags or cases in which to store or carry the iPod
- Battery duration and portable recharging options
- Accessing the controls and/or remote
- Specialty extras

In this chapter, we'll look at add-ons and third-party options that will help you perfect your mobile iPod experience. We'll also talk about the best ways to travel with your iPod—whether you're walking, driving, working out, or just on the way to work. The basic idea is to strike a good balance between your needs and conditions. If everything works together smoothly, your iPod will almost be an extension of your body, rather than an external device.

iPod headphones

The headphones (strictly speaking, "in-ear speakers") that come with the iPod are not terrible, but they're not particularly good, either.

When the MP3 format first appeared, some people thought the quality was so poor that it wasn't worth using good headphones to listen to MP3 audio. But if you listen and compare the music—especially music encoded at various bit rates—you'll see that the quality of your headphones does make a difference, especially at high volumes or in very loud or quiet areas.

The right headphones are always a good investment, no matter what you plan on using them for. Even better, you can also use them with your laptop, CD player, portable DVD player, or any other audio device. Let's examine the various options.

Open air in-ear headphones. These are the type of headphone that comes with the iPod. External sound is likely to leak inside when you're using them, but on the other hand, it can be nice to hear a bit of what's going on around you. We recommend these headphones to those who need to keep aware of their surroundings while listening to music. The headphones shown here are similar to the those that come with the iPod, but they may offer a better listening experience.

These Sennheiser MX500 headphones have a reputation for deep bass and clear high frequencies.

○
iPod
Fan Book

Isolating in-ear headphones. These headphones are shaped like earplugs and shut out external noise fairly well. For this reason, there's very little sound leakage and you can enjoy music at a high volume without annoying those around you. They also do a decent job of blocking out subway or airplane noise. You shouldn't use them for walking, however, since they amplify the sound of your steps and make it impossible to hear cars. These headphones are suitable for people who really want to focus on the sound. Apple recently introduced a set ($39) that comes with multiple caps to ensure a comfortable fit for all ear sizes.

The Audio-Technica ATH-CM5 in-ear headphone features an aluminum base alloy housing to improve the sound quality.

The Sony MDR-EX71SL has a super-micro drive that offers a superior seal. It's a popular closed-type, in-ear headphone with a comfortable fit.

Ear-attached headphones. These headphones hang over the back of each ear and fit around the back of your neck, rather than on the top of your head. Their main advantage is that you won't get tired when wearing them for hours at a time, and you can easily wear them under a baseball cap without interference. Although the in-ear phones often have better sound quality, many people prefer the fit of ear-attached headphones. They can also be quite stylish.

If you're a stickler for design, the Bang & Olufsen A8 is the headset for you. Each headphone weighs just 8 grams, so you hardly feel you're wearing them.

Over-the-ear headphones. Also called "full-size" headphones, these standard head-phones are usually the largest available. Full-size headphones come in a wide variety, including sealed (which completely cup the ear for maximum outside-noise prevention), pads (which sit on your ear), and earmuffs. Some models even fold up for easier storage. Sound quality ranges from poor to excellent, usually in tandem with price.

Active noise-canceling headphones. This type of headphone (shown below) has internal noise-canceling electronics that literally negate external noise. You can buy both in-ear and over-the-ear noise-canceling headphones. They do require a battery, and the noise-canceling digital processor degrades the sound to a certain extent. However, noise-canceling headphones are quite effective for use in places with loud, consistent noise, such as airplanes or buses.

The Sony MDR-NC11 headphones reduce outside noise dramatically, but are fairly expensive (around $100).

iPod in a case

Face it: a standard-sized iPod is too big for your pocket, especially if you're walking. The iPod mini will easily drop into a pocket, but if you want to wear the iPod on your body, you may want to consider cases and bags for maximum convenience. Options include wearing it on your neck, putting it through your belt, attaching it to the strap of your bag, and storing it in a pouch or bag.

> In the extreme cold, we recommend carrying your iPod in the inner pocket of your coat. It's fairly sensitive to temperature changes.

You can perform simple operations such as play, stop, fast-forward, rewind, and volume adjustment using the remote control (if your model comes with one), or by fumbling around in your bag. But because the remote control has no display, you'll need to use the primary controls to choose a tune, check the title of the song you're listening to, or adjust the equalization. If you constantly fiddle with your iPod settings or often peek to see what's playing, you'll want a case that allows you to see the screen and access the controls.

So, when you're shopping for bags or cases, think about how you want to use your iPod, how and where you want to carry it, and how much extra bulk you're willing to handle.

Shopping for cases

Cases are all about protection and access. The following types offer a fair amount of protection, but don't let you access the main controls or see the display. If you primarily use the remote control, consider these two.

The sleeve. High-capacity third-generation iPods (30GB and 40GB) come with this case, but owners of the new Click Wheel models will have to purchase it from Apple for $39. This case is suitable for people who access the iPod's controls less frequently, but it can be annoying if you change songs often or like to see what you're listening to.

The pouch. A pouch can protect the main body more effectively than a sleeve type case, but it's even more difficult to take the iPod out and put it back. Many pouches, such as the one sold by The Pouch (*http://www.thepouch.com/ipod.htm*), are marketed specifically for the iPod. However, since shape isn't really a factor, you can choose from a wide variety of pouches, whether designed for the iPod or not. Some pouches are quite large, and are designed to hold the iPod and all its accessories (such as headphones and a remote control).

The following cases let you operate the iPod without taking it out of the case. If you don't have a remote control for your iPod or you prefer to use the display, choose from these options.

The clear case. Belkin, MacClear, and others make clear cases specifically for the iPod. These cases let you operate your iPod through the clear plastic. Clear cases are relatively inexpensive (just $10 from MacClear) and can be attached to a bag or waistband.

The Belkin ClearCase nearly disappears from view.

The clamshell. These cases open up like a pocket organizer to display the iPod and permit access to its controls. The vertically opening type (see the next item) is easier to use than a clamshell, however, so there aren't many of these products out there. It is suitable for people who like this shape.

The Booq PodPaq014 allows for docking through the case.

The vertically opening case. Vertically opening cases are probably the easiest to operate, and can offer a sleek, professional looking design. The Booq company (*http://www.booqbags.com*) makes vertically opening cases in both nylon and leather, and iPod Armor (*http://www. ipodarmor.com*) even has one made of anodized aluminum. Since they flip open, there's nothing to interfere with the menu controls, making these cases ideal for attaching to a belt or the strap of a bag.

The silicone jacket. Silicone cases offer the most interesting variety of iPod containment options. They're based on the idea that the beauty of the white body design should not be marred by the case—although it can be altered in color, since silicon cases come in a wide range of colors, and some even glow. Best of all, they're not bulky, and they protect the iPod's body without ruining its design.

The Frogger Xskn2 silicon case is so vibrant it appears to glow in the dark.

Shopping

Where can you buy an iPod case? The following sites offer a variety of choices:

http://www.thinkdifferentstore.com

http://shopper.cnet.com

http://www.marware.com

http://www.allabouttheaccessories.com

Dealing with wires

While you're using the iPod, its various wires aren't much of a problem. When you stop using it, though, storing the remote control and headphones can be a challenge. Sure, you could just throw them into your bag willy-nilly, but the headphone cable will get tangled before you know it, and you'll be faced with the unpleasant task of unsnarling them the next time you want to listen to some tunes. Tangles can even develop when you leave the iPod lying on a table. Who wants to look at a pile of cables, no matter how pretty and white?

To deal with wires, you could use a "cable-eater." They're small, and make it convenient to reel in the cable. There's just one slight problem: the portion of the cable that it can reel in is either between the iPod and the remote control unit, or between the remote control and the headphones. They work well for adjusting the length of the remote control cable, but sometimes they don't work as well for headphone cables. Plus, with all that wire wrapped around the spool, these "cable-eaters" can quickly become "pocket-space-eaters."

The best way to control your wires is to simply whip the cables around the main body of the iPod, with the remote controller still attached. If you have Apple's iPod case with the belt clip, you can tuck the end of the wires under the clip. The only problem with this system is cosmetic—but hey, you have to put the wires somewhere!

iPod in a bag

So, you plan to carry your iPod in a bag? Here are some helpful tips:

- First, handbags don't usually make suitable cases for the iPod. Because the headphone cable must always connect to your ears (assuming you want to hear your music!), you can run into problems if the distance between your ears and the bag is too great, or if the bag sways.

- You can attach your iPod to the strap of a shoulder bag. Attaching a loop of ribbon fabric on part of the shoulder belt will hold the remote in place and make it easier to operate.

- Do you have a mobile phone case or sunglasses case? Put the iPod remote in one of those and attach it to the handle or strap of your shoulder bag. That way, if you need to, you can access the main controls without much hassle. Some cases have a handy hole through which you can pass the headphone cords. You might also try a pouch that has both belt loops and a strap loop on the back.

- Whatever your containment choice, be sure to carry the iPod in a separate compartment of a bag, or in your pocket. Do not, under any circumstances, put the iPod loosely in a bag where it will likely end up at the bottom, getting scratched and battered by the other items you're carrying (besides, it's annoying to fish the thing out).

This GAP bag includes a pouch for your iPod and a hole for headphones.

iPod in the car

The iPod can keep playing different tunes or audio books for many hours, which makes it a perfect companion for car trips. But you can't keep the headphones on all the time, so you'll need another way to get the sound from the iPod to your car stereo. Here are some possibilities.

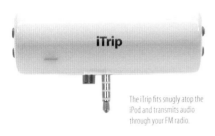

The iTrip fits snugly atop the iPod and transmits audio through your FM radio.

FM transmitters

Using an FM transmitter, such as the iTrip from Griffin Technologies (*http://www. griffintechnology.com*), you can wirelessly send iPod tunes to any FM radio. The iTrip2 costs $35, plugs into the headphone jack on the iPod, and uses FM frequencies to broadcast to your car stereo.

It's certainly convenient to play your iPod music wirelessly on your car radio (or any other stereo), but you'll find that the FM transmission process noticeably degrades sound quality. If sound quality is your main concern, you probably won't be satisfied with this solution.

⊙
iPod
Fan Book

Cassette adapters

On the other hand, you can enjoy high-quality iPod sound in your car by using a *cassette adapter*.

> For best quality, you can connect the iPod directly to audio devices using a standard headphone-plug-to-RCA cable. However, this won't work with most car stereos—unless you're lucky enough to have one with an audio input jack. In that case, all you have to do is connect your iPod with normal stereo audio cables.

Cassette adapters require you to have a cassette deck, of course, but they're extremely easy to use and produce quality results. These adapters consist of a cassette tape with a cable attached—you simply plug the cable jack into the headphone port on your iPod. Sure, the method adds a cable to your car, but the sound quality is worth it. And because cassette adapters feature a standard headphone-sized input jack, you can use them for other devices such as an MD or CD player. It can't hurt to own one and they usually cost under $20.

A car cassette adapter like this Audio Technica model
connects your iPod to your car stereo in seconds.

A few products can supply iPod power from the cigarette lighter in your car (great for *really* long road trips). The Belkin Auto Kit for iPod (which works with dockable models) sells for $49.99. Also, the ProClip (*http://www.proclipusa.com*) Dashboard Mount ($29.95, pictured below) will securely affix an iPod or an iPod mini to the dashboard of your car.

If you're lucky enough to drive a late-model BMW, you may be able to enjoy the most fully integrated iPod/auto experience by installing the BMW iPod adapter. This specialized system allows you to control your iPod through the car's audio system and multifunction steering wheel. Apple and BMW call it "the ultimate sound experience behind the wheel of the Ultimate Driving Machine," and it's certainly one of the nicest iPod accessories available. The suggested retail price is $149 plus installation charges; see *http://www.ipodyourbmw.com* for more information.

Preface

Recording
Guide

**iPod on
the Go**

The Power
of Playlists

Music
Distribution

Tips and
Tricks

iPod
Accessories

Additional
Resources

iPod
Fan Book

40

iPod on the road

One of the best things about the iPod is that you can take it with you on a trip and have all your songs on hand, without going through the trouble of choosing CDs, recording MiniDiscs, or burning CDs. But that doesn't mean you're off the hook completely—there's still some preparation required before you hit the road. In fact, carefully following these 5 cardinal rules guarantees a good traveling experience with your iPod.

❶ *Make a playlist, or a whole bunch of them*

Not all your music will be suitable for traveling, and you might not want to listen to the same album in the same order over and over. To keep yourself from tune fatigue, make at least one, and preferably multiple playlists for your trip—some for relaxing, some for drowning out crying children, some for napping during long plane rides, and so on. After all, you can combine the songs on your iPod in hundreds of different ways without taking up much memory at all.

❷ *Don't forget your charger*

Besides your headphones, remember to take along an AC adapter and the cables to connect your iPod to the adapter. Short cables save space (and the iPod uses standard ones that are relatively long), so if you travel a lot, consider replacing the one that came with the iPod. Charge the battery completely whenever possible.

❸ *Carry-on only*

Don't subject your iPod to the threat of baggage handlers or potential theft or loss. It belongs in your carry-on. Even if you're not flying, you might misplace your iPod if you put it in the large area of a big bag, mixed up with all your clothes.

❹ *Charge the battery before you go to bed*

Be sure to charge the battery before you go to bed, or if you plan on spending a few hours near a power outlet. If you charge the battery at the end of every day, you can avoid battery failures during an entire trip.

❺ *Use open-air headphones*

While sound-isolating in-ear headphones provide the best sound quality when you're stationary, they're unsuitable for travel. Even if you already own a pair for commuting, consider using open-air headphones on a trip. For one thing, they'll help you mix your sound between your surroundings and your music, especially if you're on a long-awaited journey. On a more practical note, sound-isolating headphones can cause mishaps, because you're less aware of your surroundings. But in terms of open-air headphones, the in-ear type is more suitable for travel than over-the-ear headphones or the type that clip to your ear, for one simple reason: they're much smaller and lighter.

Three handy iPod companions

Here's a selection of extras that can come in handy on trips:

❶ *Small powered speakers*

Creative TravelSound, for example, makes folding speakers that, when paired with the iPod, produce surprisingly clear, rich sound. The unit takes AA batteries, or if you're near an outlet, you can use the AC adapter instead (while you're charging your iPod).

❷ *Reading light*

The Lumatec UltraLife Reading Light, which can be used as a flashlight and a reading lamp, is indispensable for any trip. You can enjoy the nighttime stretches of the trip by reading a book while listening to the music on the iPod, without bothering your travel companions. Although there are many kinds of book lights out there, we like this one the most because of its long battery life and white light, which makes for clear text. Also, you can use it comfortably with any size book, from textbooks to paperbacks.

❸ *Largish clip*

Clip the right and left parts of your headphone cable together when stowing the iPod. This prevents the cables from getting tangled in your bag.

iPod
Fan Book

On-the-Go: a playlist of memories

The iPod's "On-the-Go Playlist" function lets you access your favorite tunes at any moment. You simply press and hold the Play/Pause button to add the song you're currently hearing to the playlist. If you have a new fourth-generation Click Wheel iPod, you can even make multiple On-The-Go Playlists. We all know that music can evoke powerful memories, so why not use this feature to your advantage? As you travel, enter songs that remind you of what you're seeing into your On-the-Go Playlists. Just keep doing this during the entire trip, whenever you feel like listening to or marking a place with a particular song.

Originally, On-the-Go playlists disappeared as soon as you synchronized your iPod to your computer. However, the latest release of iTunes lets you save On-the-Go playlists—when you dock your iPod, the playlists are now automatically saved in the same area where your other playlists live.

Be creative with the On-the-Go playlist. Whenever you have a few minutes to kill, try to think of a theme or activity and design a playlist to go with it; just remember to rename it when you next sync your iPod.

The importance of batteries

What's the biggest worry you have when traveling with the iPod? Battery life, of course. We've done some testing on the iPod's battery to provide some anecdotal evidence about such important questions as how long a battery lasts, or whether it's possible to swap out the internal battery.

How long does a battery last?

We tested a 20GB, second-generation iPod in a few different ways, after 7 months of use. The backlight was turned off to maximize battery life.

Continued playing. The battery runs out after 6 hours of use. If yours lasts less than 4 hours, you should probably think about replacing the battery (more on that later).

Intermittent service test 1. This time, we used the iPod for 90 minutes per day, starting with a full battery. It lasted for 3 days in this way. The battery ran out after 5 minutes of use on the fourth day.

Intermittent service test 2. To investigate further, we ran the iPod for 60 minutes for the first day, again starting with a full battery, and 90 minutes per day from there. The battery ran out after 30 minutes of use on the fourth day.

Not playing at all. For our final test, we left the iPod alone, turned off, with a full battery. Once a day, we pushed the "menu button" to see if the battery was still going. It ran out on the fifth day.

The most recent Click Wheel iPod touts a battery life of 12 hours (8 hours for the Mini). For full details on batteries and to learn more about keeping iPod's battery happily charged, see Apple's iPod battery page at *http://www.apple.com/batteries/ipods.html*.

Replacing the battery

Unfortunately, the iPod's battery life decreases as you use it. In some cases, you can re-vive the battery by making sure to give it a full charge a few times in a row, but if that stops working, the battery is simply getting too old. Some have said that the iPod's bat-tery will only hold a good charge for about 18 months.

So what do you do then? Battery exchange services are indispensable to long-term iPod use. If you have a valid warranty (unlikely, since the battery typically lasts much longer than most warranties), you can exchange it for free. After the warranty period expires, it costs $99 to have Apple replace it.

Some people take apart iPods by themselves to change the batteries, which is a tricky proposition and beyond the scope of this book. If you're not up to the challenge (or don't want to risk damaging your iPod), a growing number of stores and web sites will exchange the batteries for you. For example, iPodResQ.com can replace a battery in 24 hours for $79, shipping included. Without a long-lasting battery, the convenience of the iPod and its huge library rapidly decreases.

Various recharging methods

It's a good idea to keep the iPod in such a state that it can be used quickly at any time, and the best way to ensure your iPod is ready for action is to charge it as you sleep. For added convenience, you can charge your iPod's battery by connecting it to your Mac or PC. Remember, only the Click Wheel and Mini iPods can use both FireWire and USB 2.0 connections to get battery power back up. It's also easy to sync as you're hooking up your iPod for its nightly charge. Then you can rest easy, knowing that your iPod will be ready to go in the morning!

Note, however, that you can't turn off your computer or put it to sleep when charging your iPod in this manner. You must leave the computer on all night. Unfortunately, this can cause the iPod to get pretty hot, which is a good reason to stick with charging the battery using the included AC adapter. Sadly, though, the iPod comes with only one cable for charging and syncing, so you have to plug and unplug the cables out into and out of the computer all the time. Buying a spare cable helps you avoid this nuisance.

Mobile recharging

Older iPods take at least 3 hours to fully charge, which is a pretty long time. However, newer iPods have a "fast charge" feature that allows an 80% charge in two hours, and the Mini's fast charge takes only an hour. This is a great feature to use when you're on the run. Some products also allow you to power your iPod from a cigarette lighter socket, but they're primarily meant for using the iPod in a car without worrying about using the internal battery—not for recharging. The Belkin Battery Pack for iPod ($69) also allows the iPod to use 4 AA batteries instead of its internal battery.

Charging newer iPods

Older iPods require only standard FireWire cables for recharging by connecting to a computer, but Apple changed the connector to a proprietary design as part of the new docking system. So if you're buying charger accessories, be aware that many are not usable with newer iPod. If you have a newer iPod, be sure to look for the word "Dock connector" (for FireWire or USB 2.0, depending on which you use) in the product descriptions of cables and accessories.

 iPod Quick Tip

Save your battery's life

Everyone likes to have iPod on the go, but when the battery runs down, the music dies. You can make your battery last much longer between charges if you do a few simple things. For instance, turning the backlight on all the time eats up a lot of power, so set the iPod's backlight timer to go off quickly by going to Settings → Backlight timer and choosing a very small amount of time, like 2 seconds! And if you just let iPod play and don't jump around to find lots of different songs all the time, your battery will have more energy to use for music.

The Power of Playlists

Preface

Recording
Guide

iPod on
the Go

**The Power
of Playlists**

Music
Distribution

Tips and
Tricks

iPod
Accessories

Additional
Resources

iPod
Fan Book

Four rules for playlist-making

Obviously, the iPod's greatest strength is that it lets you carry around huge amounts of music. Unfortunately, the more music you have, the harder it can be to find what you're looking for. You could end up listening to only a limited number of tunes, or listening for days without getting to the one song you really want to hear. To solve these problems, jukebox and audio programs long ago introduced the *playlist*. A playlist is a powerful tool for slicing your music collection into manageable chunks, and you can create just about as many of them as you want. Since a playlist is really just a list of songs—not the songs themselves—they take up very little disk space.

Creating playlists can be troublesome and time-consuming, so we suggest the following methods, which take just a little bit of time each day.

Make a "playlist diary"

Use iTunes to make a playlist that grows little by little, whenever you listen to music on your computer, and reflects your mood at any given moment. Here's how.

First, create a new playlist. Choose a descriptive name that shows the year and the month, such as "Chill-out soundtrack for 10/2004." Now, just create a playlist as you listen, dropping in tracks you want to hear now and again. Do this whenever you listen to music on your computer, even if it's just a few tunes a day. If you make one of these each month for a year, you'll have a yearlong reflection of your feelings—it can be quite telling when you listen to it at the end of the year. Spinning this kind of playlist in shuffle mode makes a perfect accompaniment for walks around town, and keeps the songs sounding fresh because they won't always play in the same order. Best of all, it'll contain only the songs you want to hear, so there won't be any duds. Don't worry about adding the same song twice—it has no effect on the amount of free space on your iPod.

Create playlists of different lengths

For trips and other times when you want to hear a big batch of music, try creating and stashing a playlist holding, say, more than 10 hours worth of your favorite tunes. Considering an average song length of 3.5 minutes, we're talking around 200 songs here. You can start your marathon playlist at any time—just keep adding songs one after another without worrying too much about which tunes you're choosing. Once the very long playlist is complete, you can make a condensed version as a second playlist, consisting only of the songs you like a lot and want to listen to often. For the short playlist, shoot for somewhere between one and two hours in length (25 songs or so). This way, you'll have playlists for almost every circumstance—a long journey, a short commute, or just a trip to the gym.

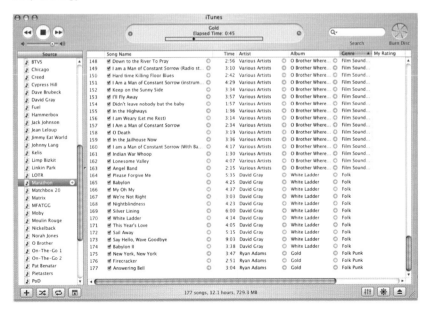

Use playlists for group outings

When you take a trip with family or friends, consider creating a playlist for each person you're traveling with. It's the modern version of a mixed tape, and it takes far less time. This way, when someone is starved for entertainment, you can just hand him your iPod with a dedicated playlist. Even if you don't end up handing over your iPod, you can burn these personalized playlists to CDs (from right within iTunes) and bring along the CDs for use in a beach boombox, rental car stereo, guest room stereo, and so on.

Build playlists by subgenre

This last rule works well if you have spoken-word recordings in your library from Audible.com, Audiobooks.org, or another source. Make a playlist for each genre, such as comedy, history, fiction, or biography. Then, if you have a hankering to listen to Japanese comic storytelling, you can easily access those files.

Save time with Smart Playlists

If you simply don't have the time or willingness to create your own playlists, don't despair. iTunes includes a "Smart Playlist" function that automatically generates playlists using a few simple parameters. If you use this function well, it's quite easy to make a playlist for your iPod without expending too much time or energy.

In addition to being easy to make, Smart Playlists have the added bonus of always updating themselves with whatever songs match your chosen criteria, even if they're imported after you've created the Smart Playlist. To make a Smart Playlist, just click File → New Smart Playlist. Then specify your criteria. You can really dig deep with your criteria, specifying anything from Artist and Genre to bit rate, the date the song was added, year, track number, your comments, and more. And that's just the beginning; you can also specify how many songs should be in the playlist and the order in which they are played.

Of course, all those choices can create their own level of confusion. To that end, here are some tips for making the most of your Smart Playlist.

Make genre-specific playlists

Just as with a regular playlist, it's a good idea to make sure your spoken-word recordings have a specified genre within iTunes, and to create playlists based on those genres. That way, your Smart Playlist will update itself to include any new songs or recordings you import that belong to the same genre.

Remember, you can type in your own genres, so you're not constricted to the ones listed in iTunes' pull-down menu. In case you forgot, you can edit a song's Genre—and all other metadata—by right-clicking (Control-click on a Mac), choosing Get Info, and clicking the Info tab.

Don't lose new tunes in the shuffle

Sometimes when you buy a new CD and import it into iTunes, you end up never playing the new songs—heck, you might even forget that you'd ever purchased them. Or maybe you're simply too lazy to track down the new tunes for listening after putting them in the iPod. The best anti-

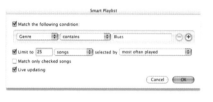

dote for this is to make a Smart Playlist that grabs *all* new tunes automatically. That way, your newest tracks will always be a few clicks away. To do so, make sure you check the box next to "Live updating" when you create a new Smart Playlist.

Automatically create a list of favorites

You can use Smart Playlists to sort songs by your own rankings. To grab only your favorite songs, find several albums by your favorite artist in iTunes, rank them with five stars in the My Rating column, then use the Smart Playlist function to create a playlist of tunes with five-star ratings. Voilà—only the hits make your list.

You can never have too many playlists

It's hard to overemphasize the importance of playlists. Make lots of them now, and continue to make new ones for as long as you own your iPod. Create lists dedicated to highly general genres, or be as specific as "songs I want to hear when I'm feeling sad," or "fast and noisy tunes," or "my all-time top 100 tracks." The third example is a favorite; you could even list your top 300 songs, but nothing more than that (you can have up to 300 tracks in a playlist). It's fairly likely that the songs in your top 100 would be the ones you'd think of listening to most often anyway.

The more playlists you have, the more likely you are to come across a song you want to hear, even when you have no particular tune in mind when you start hunting. Plus, you can even design separate playlists for two iPods and set custom syncing methods for each. For instance, if you're lucky enough to have both a white iPod and an iPod Mini, you could make the Mini into your "latest hits" jukebox by creating a 1GB Smart Playlist consisting of your most recently imported songs.

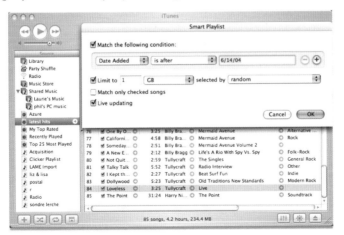

These settings will grab 1GB of songs added to the iTunes library after 6/14/2004.

Searching for songs on your iPod

Playlists and Smart Playlists can help considerably in your quest to make it easier to find songs in your iPod's vast library. But considering how many songs an iPod can hold, you can never have too many ways to group your music. To this end, you should also try to improve your searching ability with the following approaches.

Improve the browse feature through clever tagging

From your iPod's main menu, you can browse music using five of your songs' attributes: Artist, Album, Track title, Genre, and Composer. Your Album and Track lists are likely very long, and even with the iPod's speedy scroll or click wheel, it can be hard to thumb through all those entries. That's why we recommend taking advantage of all five song attributes recognized by the iPod. Try entering various descriptive words in the song's Get Info page to gain sorting options. For example, you may have overlooked the Composer attribute, but unless you listen to a lot of classical music, filling in this field can help you sort your iPod's library more effectively.

The same goes for the Genre tag. You can alter all of your songs' Genre identification, either by using the types listed in the iTunes pull-down menu or by adding your own text. Using extremely specific genres such as "New Western," "Japanese female vocalist," or "Famous standards" can help you quickly find the song (or style) you're looking for. Now, when you're out and about, you'll have two more tools for finding songs in Browse mode. But in order for it to work, you'll have to keep your iTunes library properly tagged and well organized.

More iPod organization techniques

Prune your collection

If you've never had a high-capacity MP3 player, you may assume you'll never run out of space on your iPod. But once you really start importing songs, the player will probably fill to capacity more quickly than you'd imagined! To round out this chapter, here are a few tips that will make your iPod into an efficient music machine.

Once you've been carrying your iPod around for a while, you'll get a better idea of which tunes you listen to most often, and which ones you never want to hear. If you run out of space, go through your iPod's song library in iTunes and delete the stuff you never listen to. Spare nothing: even those songs on your favorite albums that you tend to skip over. By patiently looking for these tunes and deleting them, users of the 40GB iPod can usually free up more than a gigabyte of space by doing this (4GB or 5GB iPod users should be able to free up 200MB or so).

Preface

Recording
Guide

iPod on
the Go

The Power
of Playlists

Music
Distribution

Tips and
Tricks

iPod
Accessories

Additional
Resources

◎
iPod
Fan Book

But don't kiss these songs goodbye. Put the deleted tunes together in a folder that's not part of your iTunes library, or place them in a playlist that does not autosync to your iPod. That way, those tunes will be easy to find if you want to put them back on the iPod.

Another way to reduce the number of songs on your iPod is to see which ones have a play count of zero or even one, and delete them. Scroll far enough to the right in your iTunes Library list, and you'll see a column called "Play Count." Click it, and you can scroll down to see how often you play certain songs. It's quite illuminating.

Song Name		Play Count ▾
☑ Whipping Boy	○	1
☑ Blind	○	1
☑ bonus	○	1
☑ Chicago, film score (2003): All I Care Ab...	○	1
☑ Chicago, film score (2003): Roxie	○	1
☑ Chicago, film score (2003): Class	○	1
☑ Down to the River To Pray	○	1
☑ 16 Days	○	1
☑ Turn Around	○	1
☑ Not Home Anymore	○	1
☑ 01 – Nickelback – Flat On The Floor	○	1
☑ 02 – Nickelback – Do This Anymore	○	1
☑ 03 – Nickelback – Someday	○	1
☑ 04 – Nickelback – Believe It Or Not	○	1
☑ 05 – Nickelback – Feelin Way Too Damn...	○	1
☑ 06 – Nickelback – Because Of You	○	1
☑ 07 – Nickelback – Figured You Out	○	1
☑ 08 – Nickelback – Shouldve Listened	○	1
☑ 09 – Nickelback – Throw Yourself Away	○	1
☑ 10 – Nickelback – Another Hole In The ...	○	1
☑ 11 – Nickelback – See You At The Show	○	1
☑ Martin Sexton– Glory Bound(acoustic)	○	1
☑ New Favorite	○	
☑ Let Me Touch You For Awhile	○	
☑ Stars	○	
☑ Welcome to the Cruel World	○	
☑ Forgiven	○	
☑ Waiting on an Angel	○	
☑ Roses From My Friends	○	
☑ Power of the Gospel	○	
☑ Pleasure and Pain	○	

As with all the columns in iTunes, if you want to move the Play Count column around, just click and drag it to wherever you like. We've placed it next to the Song Name column, for easy access.

Save space with playlist syncing

You can specify that iTunes should keep certain playlists updated on your iPod, so that any songs you add to those lists transfer automatically. To do so, click the iPod icon in iTunes (with the iPod plugged in), and check "Manually update these Playlists." Then select the playlists you want to update.

If you're running out of space on your iPod's disk drive, synchronizing playlists (rather than your entire iTunes library) can give you more control over what is transferred. Syncing only certain playlists is also the way to go if you want to customize the iPod's library to the maximum extent, adding only hard rock or new songs. But if you're not running out of room, stick to syncing your entire library—this comes closest to how the iPod is meant to be used (as a mobile jukebox).

If you usually sync your entire library, but have decided to switch to syncing only certain playlists, delete all the songs on your iPod before you do anything else. This will help you get rid of more stuff you don't need. Then decide which playlists you want to sync to the iPod and go from there. The playlists you choose should be large. We recommend lists such as "CDs sold after 2002" or "favorite bands."

Go multi-iPod

If you're lucky enough to own more than one iPod (say, a white iPod and an iPod Mini), try synchronizing different genres to each. It might be cool to own a rock-specific 15GB iPod, or a 4GB iPod Mini that you use only for stand-up comedy recordings. But on the other hand, you could end up either carrying extra baggage or restricting yourself to a certain genre or other slice of your collection.

It may be a better idea to use multiple iPods according to application, rather than genre: one iPod might be reserved for music you bought within the last three years, and the other could be used for older music. Since the contents of each are so clearly delineated, it's easy to choose which one you want to take with you.

Preface

Recording
Guide

iPod on
the Go

**The Power
of Playlists**

Music
Distribution

Tips and
Tricks

iPod
Accessories

Additional
Resources

iPod
Fan Book

If you already own a white iPod, you might want to pick up an iPod Mini as well. There's no reason you can't have two, and certainly many of you are drooling over the Mini. You could use the smaller Mini primarily as your daily player, with your new tunes only, and the old, larger-capacity model for oldies or long trips. Or, you could use the Mini for your favorite stuff, and the larger capacity iPod for your entire library. You could also store audiobooks or radio shows, for example, on the iPod Mini, and music on the white iPod. This technique makes it easier to use the white iPod for your party music—you can set the iPod to shuffle all songs without having to worry about starting up an entire book or recorded radio broadcast.

Get creative. If you have more than one iPod, just put a little thought into how to divide your library between the two devices; you'll thank yourself for it later.

Shuffle and Repeat in Playlist mode

If you have the latest iPod, you know that Shuffle is available right in the main menu. But on older iPods, you'll need to turn on/off both Shuffle and Repeat from the Settings menu.

There are two ways to shuffle. One is by track—in other words, to play everything on the iPod in random order. The other is by album—shuffling the tunes on each album in a row, and then proceeding to the next album. The same is true for Repeat; you can choose between a unit of tunes and a unit of albums.

On the older iPod, when you want to go back to hearing albums in order, you'll need to go back to the Menu and switch Shuffle off. Apple realized that this is pretty inconvenient—it's much easier if you could set playlists to shuffle and still play albums in order, as you can on the newer iPod models. And in the meantime, many other players are still simply *unable* to play albums in order, so we certainly shouldn't complain too much.

Music Distribution

Preface

Recording
Guide

iPod on
the Go

The Power
of Playlists

**Music
Distribution**

Tips and
Tricks

iPod
Accessories

Additional
Resources

iPod
Fan Book

62

Doing more with playlists

The iPod's the best machine you can buy for playing back music on the go, but sooner or later you'll have to learn how to set your tunes free so they can be sent to friends, played on your stereo, and archived to prevent the loss of your music library.

In this chapter, we'll show you how to save and organize playlists in iTunes, share them with your friends, and use cheap optical media to back up your collection.

Saving playlists

Now that you've spent all that time creating playlists, you'll be happy to know you can do a lot more than just listen to them. In fact, the power of the playlist extends well beyond the iPod itself. For example, the playlists you've created in iTunes are automatically saved, which, among other things, gives you an easy way to back up your iPod's playlists. Playlists also give you a repository in your iTunes library for songs you specifically *don't* want to sync with your iPod, either because its space is nearly maxed out, or because you've decided that you don't want to hear them when you're out and about. The third extra function of saved playlists is to send them to other people.

Exporting song lists from playlists

iTunes provides several ways for you to share both your music and your taste. If you have a friend with a similar music library, for example, you can actually send a saved playlist—but not the songs themselves. To send a playlist, choose File → Export Song List. You can save the file as either a text (*.txt*) or XML (*.xml*) file. We recommend saving them as text files, because they're easier to deal with.

Playlist-sharing in this form isn't too common, because the recipient has to have all of the same songs in his collection in order to be able to hear them. If he does have the same songs (perhaps you have very similar taste in music), he simply needs to choose File → Import and select the text file you've sent him.

Doesn't sound so bad? There's a hitch: the recipient must have those songs with the exact same *ID3 tags* (song information) on the files. If you both ripped the songs from CD and used the default song information, or bought the songs from the iTunes Music Store, you won't encounter any problems. But if you downloaded the songs from a filesharing service or edited the tags yourself, the recipient may need to perform some reconstruction work on the playlist so that the iPod knows where the listed songs reside. All of this can be clunky, and it's not something most beginners or computer neophytes will want to tackle.

Still, sharing playlists in this manner can make sense for fans of the same music and those who own many of the same albums. For example, you and a friend could exchange playlists consisting of what you each consider to be a favorite artist's 20 best songs.

Sharing playlists on a network

There's an easier way to share playlists if you use iTunes on a local network (either at work or in your home). Using Apple's Rendezvous networking technology, you can share your music within a local network so that other people on the same network can view and play (but not download, of course) your tunes. To share your music, click iTunes → Preferences → Sharing. You can search for others' shared libraries, share all of your music, or just choose selected playlists to share.

Network sharing works only between users of the same version of iTunes.

Publishing playlists

If you're really, really proud of your playlist, you can go beyond just sharing it with friends and coworkers. You can actually publish your playlists to the iTunes Music Store, for everyone to evaluate. To publish a completed playlist, highlight it in the iTunes list, and click the little right-pointing arrow that appears.

Once you click the arrow and enter your iTunes ID and password, iTunes will search for the music in your playlist and show you which songs are available for download from the Music Store. Your published *iMix*, as it's called, will include only these songs. iTunes also creates a custom image for your playlist, based on album covers. Click Publish, and you're done.

Your published iMix will show up on the iTunes Music Store (just click the large iMix button in the middle of the Music Store home page), with the total number of songs, as well as a handy "buy-all" button that includes the price for all the songs in the mix. Of course, what good are public playlists if you can't rate them? Each iMix also includes a rating scale, and you can sort public playlists by rating. Apple provides a URL that you can email to any iTunes user, so they'll have a chance to browse, preview, and buy the songs on your list.

Archive tunes to CD or DVD

So far we've talked about sharing your playlists, saving them for posterity, and showing them to the public. That's not the end of what you can do with your tunes, though, and the iPod isn't the only way to make them portable. If you're looking for a way to back up your music files (including their playlist order), consider burning them onto optical media, such as CDs or DVDs.

Why would you do this, especially if you own the original CDs? Well, for one thing, it's a lot of work to reconvert an entire library from CD to MP3 or AAC. Burning your library to CD or DVD also makes it easy to migrate your library to a new machine; just remember to *deauthorize* the old one within the iTunes Music Store first, so that any songs purchased from Apple will be sure to play on your new machine. To deauthorize, click Advanced → Deauthorize Computer. You can play purchased iTunes music on up to five authorized computers.

iTunes can burn media files directly to data CD-R/RW discs and DVDs, so it's easy to make backups straight from within the program. To burn a CD using iTunes, insert a blank disc and click File → Burn Playlist to Disc. iTunes provides two types of burn to choose from: Data and Audio. For archiving MP3s and AACs (for posterity or transport to a new machine), you should always choose Data. For burning CDs that you want to play on a stereo, choose the CD type of Audio (simple CD rips), and follow the instructions through the burning process.

If you burn audio CDs, they'll play on just about any CD player, which is a great way for you to let other people listen to the tunes you enjoy on your iPod. Just don't give out the CDs, as you could be committing copyright infringement. You can also move your songs onto devices that need to record audio in real time, such as certain Minidisc players. If you're planning on burning your playlist as an audio CD, make sure it's the right length to fit onto one CD-R.

iPod
Fan Book

Connect your iPod to your stereo

So, what if you have some great playlists stored on your iPod that could really be the life of the party? You could pass the iPod around the room and let everyone have a listen on the headphones. Or you could connect your iPod to your stereo and broadcast the tunes in hi-fi. The only way to connect first-generation iPods to a stereo is to use their headphone ports, but making the connection with newer iPods is far easier: their docking cradles have a line-out port that bypasses your iPod's volume circuitry and offers an even cleaner sound.

The best thing about the iPod's compatibility with home stereo systems is that you can use the iPod in places where it's either impossible or expensive to connect your computer to your stereo, such as the living room or a basement party room. You could even use powered speakers (the ones with a built-in amplifier that plug into a wall outlet) to make the iPod the core of your audio entertainment system.

From its design, it's apparent that JBL had the iPod in mind when it created the Creature 2.1 Speaker line. It looks great with the iPod, and pumps out pretty big sound from its subwoofer and two satellites.

One caveat: while iPod-stereo combinations can sound very good, neither the MP3 format nor the iPod's hardware was designed with extremely high-end stereos in mind. For this reason, you shouldn't use the iPod as part of an audiophile sound system (audiophile components generally cost $10,000 and up, and should be used only with other audiophile-level devices).

Preface

Recording
Guide

iPod on
the Go

The Power
of Playlists

**Music
Distribution**

Tips and
Tricks

iPod
Accessories

Additional
Resources

◎
iPod
Fan Book

Transferring tunes to another computer

The iPod is made for use with a single computer. However, there are times when you need to upload songs from your iPod to a second computer: one obvious (and legal) reason is to back up your music files, or include your music library on both your home and work computer. Transferring music to a second computer takes a little tweaking, since Apple includes some copyright protection tools. However, you can circumvent those tools with relative ease. Please note, however, that we're not advocating copyright infringement in any way—giving your music files to your friends is not legal, and you should be aware of copyright issues before you proceed.

With Windows

If you want to copy the music data from the iPod into a Windows environment, begin by clicking Start → Settings → Control Panel → Folder Options and, under the View tab, click "Show hidden files and folders." This option allows Windows to see the hidden folders on the iPod where the music lives. For this method to work, however, you must enable disk mode in iTunes—with your iPod plugged in, click the iPod icon at the bottom of the iTunes window to open iPod Preferences. Check the box next to "Enable disk use." Your iPod will then mount as a drive and you can drag files to and from it.

If you're looking for something a little more full-featured, try Anapod Explorer, an excellent iPod syncing program from Red Chair (*http://redchairsoftware.com*) that's like a supercharged iTunes for advanced users. Aside from allowing you to grab songs off of an iPod, it lets you do even more "out there" stuff, such as viewing your library through a web browser and transferring files onto the iPod via drag-and-drop.

With a Mac

You can manually transfer song files to and from your iPod and a second computer, but you'll have to be able to see them first. Normally, iTunes hides your music library in hidden folders on the Mac so that you can't simply mount the iPod as a disk on any computer and drag files to and from it. However, Mac OS X has a function that lets you view the iPod's hidden folders when the device is mounted as an external FireWire drive. To mount the iPod as an external drive, plug in the iPod, click the iPod icon at the bottom of the iTunes window to open iPod Preferences, and check the box next to "Enable disk use." The iPod will show up in your Finder window as a regular drive, similar to a hard drive or a CD. Once you can view the music in the iPod's hidden folders, you can drag files to and from it. You can also use a program called ResEdit (*http://resexcellence.com*) to view your hidden folders, or you can look for programs designed specifically for transferring music from your iPod, such as InitGraf Software's iPodViewer (*http://homepage. mac.com/initgraf*).

iPodViewer lets you transfer files directly to or from your iPod.

Preface

Recording
Guide

iPod on
the Go

The Power
of Playlists

**Music
Distribution**

Tips and
Tricks

iPod
Accessories

Additional
Resources

○
iPod
Fan Book

70

Using the iPod as a hard drive

Your iPod is more than a music player—it can be used as an external USB or FireWire hard drive. USB 2.0 and FireWire offer a fast connection, so you can speedily move large files onto or off of the iPod. You can even use it as a boot drive for Mac or Windows, meaning you can install a version of your operating system on the iPod (this process is somewhat difficult on a PC) and then use it to start your computer. If you're using your iPod as a portable hard disk, you'll need to enable disk mode in iTunes before the iPod will show up on your desktop (on a Windows machine it'll appear in "My Computer").

> If you transfer large files between your Mac and PC, sync primarily with the PC. Both PCs and Macs recognize Windows-based iPods, but a Windows machine can't see a Mac-synced iPod unless you use a utility such as Mediafour's XPlay 2 (*http://www.mediafour.com/products/xplay/*).

If you need to move really large files, *initialize* your iPod first, in order to delete everything quickly. To do this on a PC, click Start → Programs → iPod Updater (the version depends on your iPod model). On a Mac, it's in Applications → Utilities → iPod Software Updater. Click the Restore button to erase your iPod and return it to the factory settings. You'll then be prompted to initialize your iPod. Once you do so, you'll have a clean, empty iPod. Transfer the files to it, and when you attach your iPod to your primary computer again, the music will sync back onto it. This is sort of a hassle—if you plan on often using your iPod as a hard drive, it helps to own one with a large capacity (20GB, at the very least).

Transform your iPod into a PDA

While the iPod does music best of all, it also has more extra features than other MP3 players out there: text file support, an address book, games, and more. Here, we'll cover the iPod's extra functions—located conveniently in the Extras menu. Thanks to Apple's well-thought-out design, many of the items in the Extras menu are self-explanatory. We'll just cover the clever stuff.

Reading text with the iPod

The latest iPods include a Notes function that allows you to read text files as a standard feature. Even if you can't imagine reading an entire book on the screen, you can still use this feature to store short notes to yourself or clippings from the Web (directions from MapQuest.com, lyrics, recipes, workout plans, etc.).

If you do decide that you'd like to read a book or two on the go, many electronic editions (e-books) are available. After downloading them to your iPod, you can casually read a new book whenever (and wherever) you have the time.

Older iPods can still read text, but you'll need a program such as Podtext (free, *http://homepage.sunrise.ch/mysunrise/thhdesign/more.html*) to transfer text files to the iPod's Contacts menu. Or, you could just get a newer iPod!

My Workout
3 sets; 10-12 reps each:
Bicep curl (15 lbs)
Tricep kick back (10 lbs)
Incline bench press (50 lbs)
Hamstring curl (65 lbs)
Lunges (holding 20 lbs)
Calf raises (25 lbs)

Useful sites for finding e-books

If the data you download is in text format, you can read not only short memos but also long passages. Here are some sites where you can download free e-books and other text files to read on your iPod. In most cases, you can browse them by author, title, subject, or genre.

- Authorama: *http://www.authorama.com*
- Creative Commons: *http://commoncontent.org*
- Literature.org: *http://www.literature.org*
- Project Gutenberg: *http://www.gutenberg.net*
- Upenn's digital book library: *http://onlinebooks.library.upenn.edu/lists.html*

Try searching Google or your favorite search engine, too—you'll find all sorts of free text available online.

LyriPod

Books aren't the only thing you can read on your iPod. If you want to sing along to your favorite songs but can't always remember the words, LyriPod (*http://nu.gg/lyripod*) is the program for you. Simply select a song on your iPod and LyriPod will try to find its lyrics online. It then automatically downloads any found lyrics to a Lyrics subfolder under the Notes menu.

The iPod Address Book

In this day and age, everyone seems to have a cell phone, and most of them can store contacts. So, the address list may not be the iPod's most essential feature. However, it may still be worth loading contacts on the iPod in case your cell phone battery dies. Alternatively, you can whittle down your contact list to about 10 essential entries, so the iPod can act as an emergency backup in case you lose your phone. If you really want to load up the iPod with your personal information—including email, tasks, contacts, and iCal entries—consider third-party software, such as iPod-It ($14.95, *http://www.zapptek.com/ipod-it/*).

Contacts	
Dana Connelly	>
Emma Cashman	>
Josh Maric	>
Naomi Cleary	>
Tracy O'Neal	>
Vinnie DeLano	>

The iPod Calendar

Your iPod also has a built-in Calendar, which can import appointments from many different calendar programs and formats. You can even keep separate calendars for work and personal use. It's easy to keep your iPod Address Book and Calendar synced with your Mac's Address Book and iCal—just use Apple's iSync.

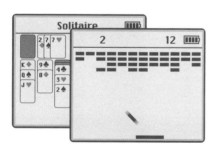

Games

Your iPod also comes with a few fun games (Brick, Parachute, Music Quiz, and Solitaire) to help pass the time.

Boosting the iPod's powers

In this section, you'll find more tidbits that will help you use the Internet and iTunes to maximize your iPod's lofty potential. Although it's just a small sample, it may prove useful.

The Apple iTunes Music Store

As you probably know, Apple has a music store inside iTunes, where you can choose from a vast and growing catalog of music that you can purchase and download. You can find the iTunes Music Store (iTMS) near the top of the column on the left edge of the iTunes program. When you're connected to the Internet (DSL and cable users don't need to worry about this), you can click it to bring up the iTMS screen in the main area of iTunes.

Search by Artist or Album in the search box at the upper-right of the screen if you know what you're looking for. But if you skip everything else on the page, you're missing out. Take the time to explore the iMix section, which consists of playlists just like those we discussed in Chapter 4. Who knows, if you submit your iMix, it may someday reach the top-rated section! Apple is constantly experimenting with new ways to present digital music in its store, so it could be worth touring this page every once in awhile. There's no "you break it you buy it" policy, so you can't hurt anything by looking around—you can even listen to a 30-second sample of any song you find in the store, without entering a credit card. If you decide to buy a song, click the Buy button to its right. Then follow the next few screens to set up an account.

Once you enter your credit card and other information (Apple keeps it secure), you can buy the song and it'll download right into your iTunes library—easy as can be. Songs from iTMS are encoded in the secure AAC format, at 128 kbps. The FairPlay protection Apple wraps around songs sold in its store means it'll play on your computer, your iPod, and up to four other computers (for a total of five). Authorizing the other computers is easy—just try playing a purchased AAC file on one of them after installing iTunes, and follow the instructions. One benefit of buying music online instead of downloading from sporadic sources is that all the track information is correct, so the tracks integrate seamlessly into iTunes and your iPod.

iTunes tips for the iPod

The iPod's operation is easy to grasp, but somehow there are always more things to learn, even without the use of third-party software add-ons. For instance, here are three things iTunes can do that you may not have known about.

❶ *Use the context menu cleverly*

While looking at any song list in iTunes, you can sort it just like you would in a normal Mac or Windows folder: by clicking one of the criteria at the top of the list (Song Title, Time, Artist, Album, Genre, My Rating, and Last Played). That's a lot of options, but there are more. Select your library or the playlist you wish to add sorting options to, and then go to Edit → View Options. You'll see a big chart where you can check off various options. At the very least, you should consider adding Date Added, so you can easily track down newly acquired songs.

View Options

♪ Spacklin' Playlist

Show Columns

☑ Album	☑ Genre
☑ Artist	☐ Kind
☐ Beats Per Minute	☑ Last Played
☐ Bit Rate	☑ My Rating
☐ Comment	☑ Play Count
☐ Composer	☐ Sample Rate
☑ Date Added	☐ Size
☐ Date Modified	☑ Time
☐ Disc Number	☐ Track Number
☐ Equalizer	☐ Year

OK   Cancel

❶

Preface

Recording
Guide

iPod on
the Go

The Power
of Playlists

Music
Distribution

**Tips and
Tricks**

iPod
Accessories

Additional
Resources

iPod
Fan Book

❷

❸

❷ *Archive your library using XML*

In case anything happens to your careful organization of iTunes tracks—say, someone messes up all the playlists—it's a good idea to archive your library's organizational setup every once in a while. You can also use this method to save different musical profiles.

To archive your library, go to File → Export Library and save the library in XML format. To restore your iTunes settings (or apply them to one of your other authorized iTunes computers) select File → Import to reload your library structure.

❸ *Trim your iPod's collection as you would a Bonsai tree*

There will be times when you will want to reconsider the tunes you have in your iPod, because it's filled to capacity. When this happens, the best way to edit your selection is to create a new playlist—called something like "iPod songs." Drag playlists, albums, songs, etc. into this new playlist. You can always see how much memory your iPod-dedicated playlist consumes at the bottom of the iTunes screen.

Try sorting the lists in different ways, and you'll probably find lots of duplicates—for instance, songs from the original album, the EP, the B-side, and the greatest hits album. Obviously, you should also look for stuff you never feel like listening to when you're out and about. If you truly run out of tracks to cut, your final resort is to reduce compression on songs. Keep adding and subtracting until the playlist is a few megabytes underneath your iPod's maximum capacity.

After that's done, right-click (Control-click on a Mac) the iPod in iTunes's left column, choose iPod Options, and switch the updating method to "Automatically update selected playlists only." Select only the playlist you just created, the one specifically for iPod songs.

Now you can play around with your new playlist as much as you want, making sure it never takes up more space than your iPod has. If you're really into playlists, you can even create a bunch of small ones that add up to just under your iPod's capacity, then specify that they should be automatically updated. However, if you decide to do this, only those tracks will sync to the iPod when you click File → Update songs.

iPod Preferences

○ Automatically update all songs and playlists
⦿ Automatically update selected playlists only:

☐ Top 25 Most Played
☐ baps
☐ dingle Selection
☑ for ipod
☐ test mp3s

○ Manually manage songs and playlists

☑ Open iTunes when attached
☑ Enable disk use
☐ Only update checked songs

[OK]   [Cancel]

Preface

Recording
Guide

iPod on
the Go

The Power
of Playlists

Music
Distribution

**Tips and
Tricks**

iPod
Accessories

Additional
Resources

iPod
Fan Book

Turn your iPod into a news machine

The world is a busy place, but you can have iPod keep you informed! You can find many programs on the Web that will download news updates and other reading from the Internet right to your iPod so you can catch up with the world while you listen to music. A good news program with lots of options for Mac OS X is Pod2Go at *http://www.kainjow.com/pod2go*. If you use Windows, try EphPod at *http://www.ephpod.com* for news, movie listings, and weather reports.

iPod Accessories

iPod
Fan Book

iPod accessories

The iPod has more available accessories than most other Apple products. Evidently, both the device's function and its design compel manufacturers to make accessories and consumers to buy them.

iPod owners should buy what they want, obviously, but it's important to keep in mind the distinction between "must items" and "maniac items." One must-have item, though, is a product called iPod Wheel Film. This is a sticker you put on the scroll wheel to protect it, and it comes in many varieties, from pure white to various designs. It protects the wheel from dirt and so forth, and at the same time decorates the iPod smartly. It's also inexpensive, and creates a better, more textured surface on the scroll wheel. The following pages offer some other suggestions.

The iPod Wheel Film. A scroll wheel gets pretty dirty since fingers rub it, so a protective sticker like this one can keep yours clean. There are many fun designs from which to choose.

❶ *Infrared remote control unit*

The TEN naviPod (*http://www.tentechnology.com*) includes an infrared remote control and receiver that let you control the iPod's basic functions from across the room. It's extremely handy to have when the iPod is attached to your stereo system. The naviPod costs $49 and works with both the original and new iPod types.

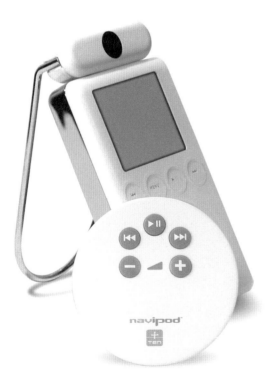

The naviPod set lets you control your iPod's basic functions from across the room.

❷ *Headphone splitter*

You can find adapters at many electronics stores that turn one
headphone jack into two, which is nice if you're traveling with
a companion and you both want to listen to the same song
or audiobook. They're cheap, too (usually less than $10).

❸ *Griffin Technology iTrip*

As mentioned earlier, the iTrip is an excellent FM transmitter for the iPod. The sen-
sitivity and the sound quality aren't as good as the best larger FM transmitters, but
it more than makes up for that because it has such a high sense of design. The iTrip
integrates nicely with the iPod and iTunes, allows you to choose from a wide range of
transmitting frequencies, and has the ability to save settings.

❹ *CD burner*

You might find yourself with music in formats that can't be transferred to the iPod.
In some cases (especially when you bought the tunes from an unsupported online
music store), the only recourse you have is to burn the tracks onto an audio CD, and
then re-rip them back into iTunes so you can load them onto your iPod. A CD-burning
optical drive is a solid investment, and you can get a cheap one for less than $50.

The Belkin Voice Recorder

Thanks to the appearance of the Belkin Voice Recorder for iPod ($34.95; for docking iPods only), it's now possible to use the iPod to record voice memos in mono. Unless sound quality isn't important, don't bother using it to record music, but for quick voice notes, the Belkin Voice Recorder works extremely well.

It's also easy to use. To prepare the iPod for recording, all you have to do is detach your iPod's headphones and connect the Voice Recorder. It's as simple to use as a dedicated voice recorder (but who needs one of those these days?). Interestingly enough, Belkin managed to cram not only a microphone and analog-to-digital converter into this adapter, but also a tiny speaker! This means you can play back voice memos instantly. The other handy thing about this attachment is that it derives all of its power from your iPod, so there's no battery to change.

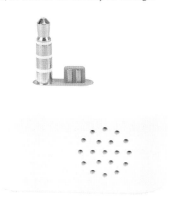

And as with the On-the-Go playlists, voice recordings import into iTunes automatically upon the next sync.

If your iPod has a lot of free space, you could try stuff like recording what's going on in a room all day long, but your battery probably lasts about six hours at a maximum (although you could use the power adapter to extend this), and you'd have to listen to the whole thing back again in order to hear what happened. Besides, the iPod is too friendly a device to be used for something as dodgy as surveillance.

Preface

Recording
Guide

iPod on
the Go

The Power
of Playlists

Music
Distribution

Tips and
Tricks

**iPod
Accessories**

Additional
Resources

iPod
Fan Book

86

The Belkin Media Reader

If you're the kind of person who doesn't need to cram music into every byte of your iPod, its ability to function as an external hard drive is very attractive. When the iPod first came out, its data storage function was useful only when there was a PC or Mac around, so that you could upload or download your data. But then came Belkin Media Reader for the iPod. This product makes the iPod into something of a peripheral for your digital camera, so you can store your camera's photos on the iPod without using a computer. The ramifications of this are awesome—basically, it means that you can go on trips without a laptop, since the iPod handles storage.

Ah, you say, but how can this thing work with all of the various types of flash storage out there? The answer is that the Belkin Media reader is big—as in bigger than the iPod. That's the only way it could be designed to handle SD/MMC cards, SmartMedia cards, CompactFlash (Types 1 and 2), or even a Memory Stick.

The Media Reader is light and clearly well designed—if you take a lot of digital pictures, you should definitely pick one up. The only drawback is that it can import data only from digital cameras; the ability to grab any kind of data from any type of card and put it on the iPod would be a welcomed additional feature.

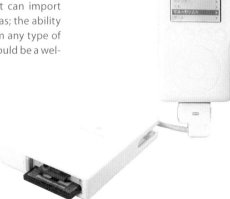

Additional Resources

Preface

Recording
Guide

iPod on
the Go

The Power
of Playlists

Music
Distribution

Tips and
Tricks

iPod
Accessories

Additional
Resources

Sites and stops for iPod info

The Apple web site provides tons of information about the iPod. In addition to offering descriptions of the iPod and its accessories, it contains a guide describing how you can get the most out of your iPod.

- Apple's iPod site: *http://www.apple.com/ipod*
- Apple's iPod support site: *http://www.apple.com/support/ipod*
- Apple's battery replacement program: *http://www.apple.com/support/ipod/service/battery.html*

Of course, it's possible to buy an iPod on the Web.

- Apple store: *http://store.apple.com*

As you would expect, given the popularity of the iPod, there are various other sites in addition to Apple's, both large and small, which offer information about the device. These generally consist of iPod rumors, tips, and news. If you're interested in getting the latest accessories and advice for your little musical friend, they've got you covered.

- iPod Lounge: *http://www.ipodlounge.com*
- iPoding: *http://ipoding.com*
- Everything iPod: *http://www.everythingipod.com*
- CNET: *http://www.cnet.com*
- XtremeMac: *http://www.xtrememac.com*
- Apple's own accessory site: *http://www.apple.com/ipod/accessories.html*

If you're interested in learning about headphones, the site below offers lots of detailed information.

- Headphones.com: *http://www.headphones.com*

iPod applications and tools

As an iPod owner, you definitely need to know about Apple's software update page. This is where you can find *firmware* (sort of like the iPod's operating system) updates that can increase battery life, fix bugs, add features, and all sorts of other fun stuff.

http://www.apple.com/ipod/download

And in case you want to find the latest version of iTunes, it's always here.

http://www.apple.com/itunes

Software for Mac

Apple's own iTunes is the easiest way to manage music on an iPod, but using third-party software can give you special syncing powers. Here's our favorite one for the Macintosh (for more apps, check out iPodLounge.com).

• Panic Audion (for OS 8.5-X): *http://www.panic.com/audion*

Next, let's discuss MP3 encoders. The Blacktree encoder listed here is for LAME format—you may find that you get a better sound by switching to it. See the section on alternate encoders in Chapter 1 for more information. The BPM Inspector is a tool for measuring a song's beats-per-minute by clicking a mouse in time with the music. You can use this number to add the BPM information to your songs' ID3 tags, for better Smart Playlists.

• Blacktree iTunes-LAME Encoder: *http://blacktree.com/apps/iTunes-LAME*

• Blacktree iTunes-BPM Inspector: *http://blacktree.com/apps/iTunes-BPM*

If you want to record streaming broadcasting on the Internet, we recommend the following two products.

• StreamRipper (Mr. Wai [Simon] Liu): *http://streamripper.sourceforge.net*

• RadioLover (Bitcartel Software, shareware $15): *http://www.bitcartel.com/radiolover*

Preface

Recording
Guide

iPod on
the Go

The Power
of Playlists

Music
Distribution

Tips and
Tricks

iPod
Accessories

Additional
Resources

StreamRipper is open source software (*http://www.opensource.org*), which has amassed a large fan-base. RadioLover is based on this program and is slightly easier to use, but it costs $15 and up (depending on which version you pick).

Software for PC

Windows iTunes replaced the difficult-to-use MusicMatch program, so Windows users now know the joy of syncing an iPod with iTunes. But again, third-party software is still worth looking at for special features:

- Red Chair Anapod Explorer: *http://www.redchairsoftware.com/anapod*
- EphPod (Joe Masters): *http://www.ephpod.com*
- MediaFour Xplay: *http://www.mediafour.com*

Anapod offers some great extra features—you can even use it to make the iPod's library into an automatically generated web page, accessible from anywhere in the world. But if you have some extra time, browse the sites of the others to see what they have to offer.

Using the iTunes built-in codec is easy, but again, many experts believe that using the LAME codec results in better-sounding results. There are many ways to use LAME for ripping CDs to MP3 on Windows, but these two options are the best. See Chapter 1 for more information on alternative encoders for Windows:

- CDex: *http://cdexos.sourceforge.net*
- Exact Audio Copy: *http://www.exactaudiocopy.de*

Finally, for recording streams on a Windows machine, try the following program. It can split recordings automatically into separate MP3s, and will even label some of them with the proper ID3 tags:

- Replay Radio: *http://www.replay-radio.com*

Index